This is a book about the UNIVERSE, and other Very Big Things. So it uses Very Big Numbers - even MILLIONS and BILLIONS.

To remind you just how big those numbers are, first try counting to a smaller number - ONE HUNDRED. At normal speed, that should take about one minute. Keep counting, and you'll reach a THOUSAND in about 12 minutes.

If you decide to continue counting to a MILLION, don't plan on doing anything else for a while. Counting for a steady 10 hours a day, it will take about 3 weeks.

If you are REALLY ambitious and would like to count on to a BILLION, you'd better make that your career. Counting 12 hours a day, it will take you more than 50 years!

This book has some HUNDREDS and THOUSANDS, and LOTS of MILLIONS and BILLIONS. Will it give you big ideas? You can count on it!

IS A BLUE WHALE
THE BIGGEST THING THERE IS?

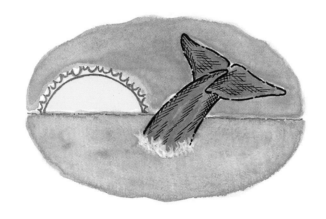

Robert E. Wells

FRANKLIN WATTS
LONDON•SYDNEY

This edition 2005

First published in the UK by Franklin Watts,
338 Euston Road, London, NW1 3BH

Franklin Watts Australia
Level 17/207 Kent Street, Sydney, NSW 2000

First published by Albert Whitman & Company,
Morton Grove, Illonois, USA

Text and illustrations © 1993 Robert E. Wells
Notes and activities © 2005 Franklin Watts

A CIP catalogue record is available from the British Library.
Dewey Classification 530.8

Printed in Singapore

ISBN 978 0 7496 6222 6

Franklin Watts is a division of Hachette Children's Books,
an Hachette Livre UK company.

This is the tail of a blue whale.
The "flipper" parts are called flukes.

Just the flukes, all by
themselves, are bigger than
most of Earth's creatures.

Here's the WHOLE blue whale. It's not just bigger than MOST of Earth's creatures, it's bigger than ALL of them.

A blue whale can grow to be 30 metres long and weigh 150 tonnes!
It's the biggest animal that ever lived.

But of course, a blue whale is NOT
The Biggest Thing There Is.

If you put 100 blue whales in a really big jar,

and then put two of those whale jars on an enormously large platform,

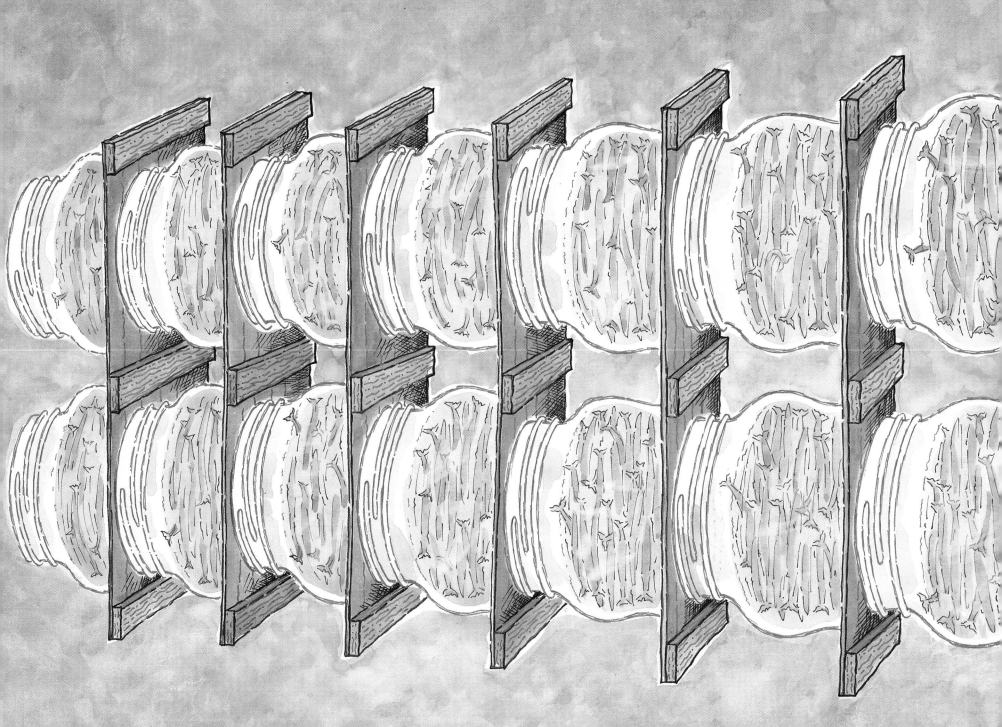

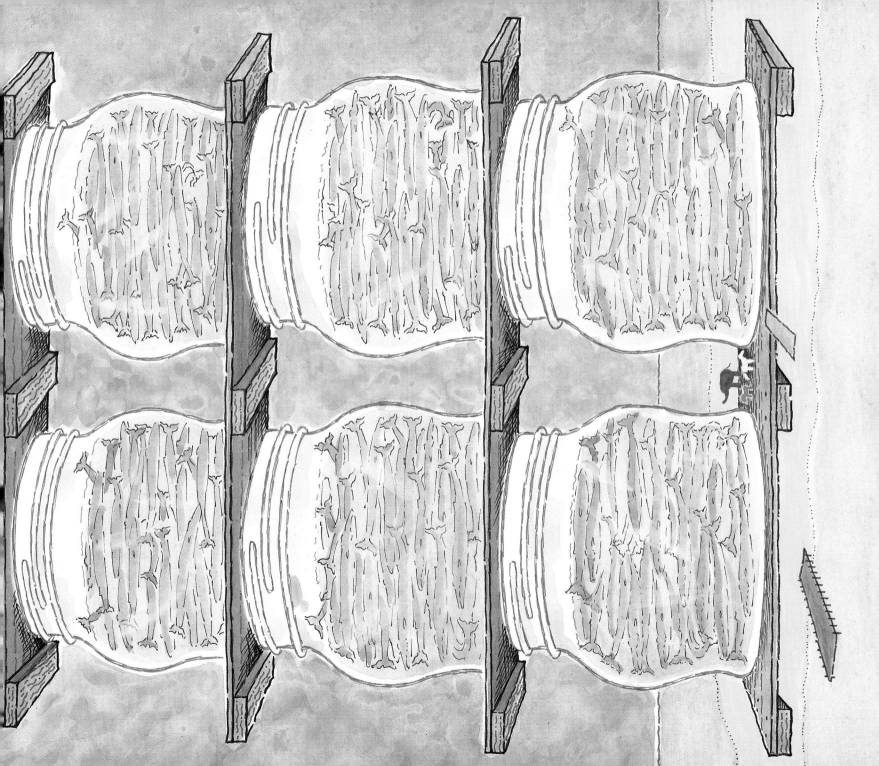

and then made a tremendously tall tower
out of 10 platforms of whale jars,

11

that tower of whale jars would look quite small
balanced on top of Mount Everest!

Yes, Mount Everest is certainly big. If it were hollow, it could hold millions of whale jars.

But it's not even CLOSE to being The Biggest Thing There Is.

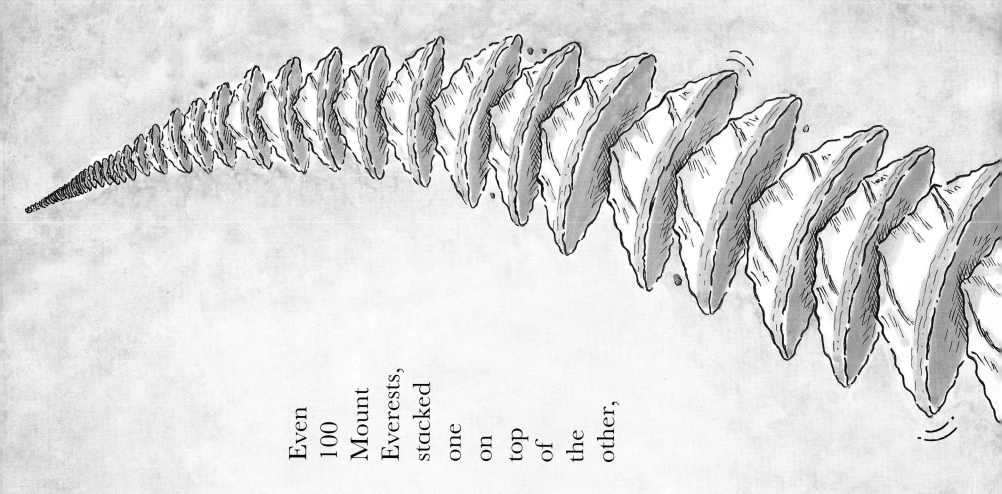

Even
100
Mount
Everests,
stacked
one
on
top
of
the
other,

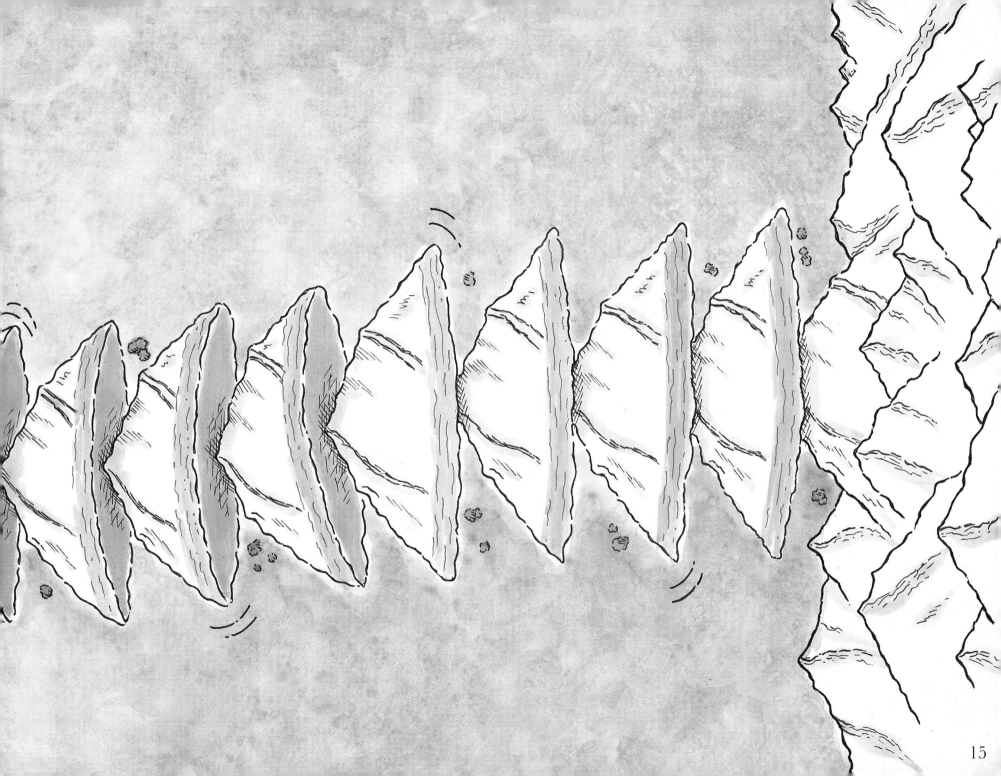

would be a mere WHISKER on the face of the Earth!

And just in case you thought our EARTH was the
BIGGEST THING THERE IS,

here are
100
full-sized
Earths,
in a
rather
large bag,

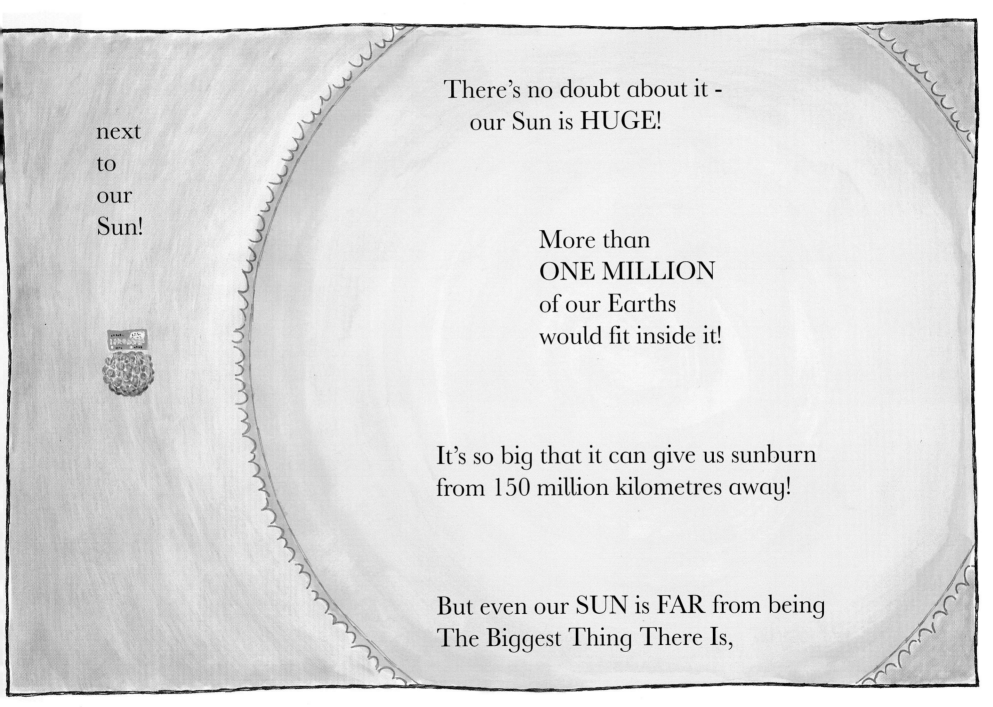

next
to
our
Sun!

There's no doubt about it -
our Sun is HUGE!

More than
ONE MILLION
of our Earths
would fit inside it!

It's so big that it can give us sunburn
from 150 million kilometres away!

But even our SUN is FAR from being
The Biggest Thing There Is,

because
if our Sun
were turned
into a
**SUN-SIZED
ORANGE,**

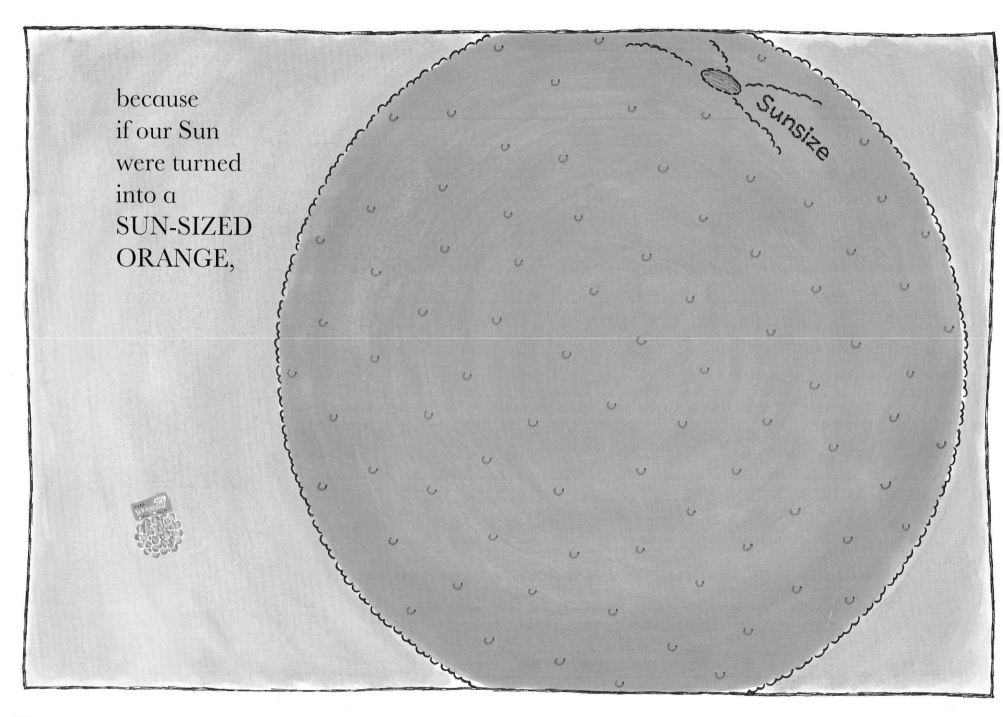

and packed in an IMMENSE orange crate
along with 99 other Sun-sized oranges,

100
SUN-SIZED
ORANGES
"A TASTE of FIRE in EVERY BITE"

it could be set on top of something
much bigger - a red supergiant
star called ANTARES!

Stars come in many different sizes.
Our Sun and Antares are both stars,
but our Sun is medium-sized, and
Antares is... well, it's a SUPERGIANT!

Antares was not always this big. All stars
have lifetimes, and some, like Antares, expand
to enormous sizes and turn red as they get
close to the end of their lives.

Antares has grown so big that
MORE THAN FIFTY MILLION OF
OUR SUNS WOULD FIT INSIDE IT!

How could anything be that big?

How could anything be BIGGER?

Our galaxy, the MILKY WAY, is much, MUCH bigger. A galaxy is a gathering of a great number of stars. The MILKY WAY is made up of BILLIONS of stars, including Antares. Along with those stars, there are countless comets and asteroids, lots of meteors, and at least nine planets!

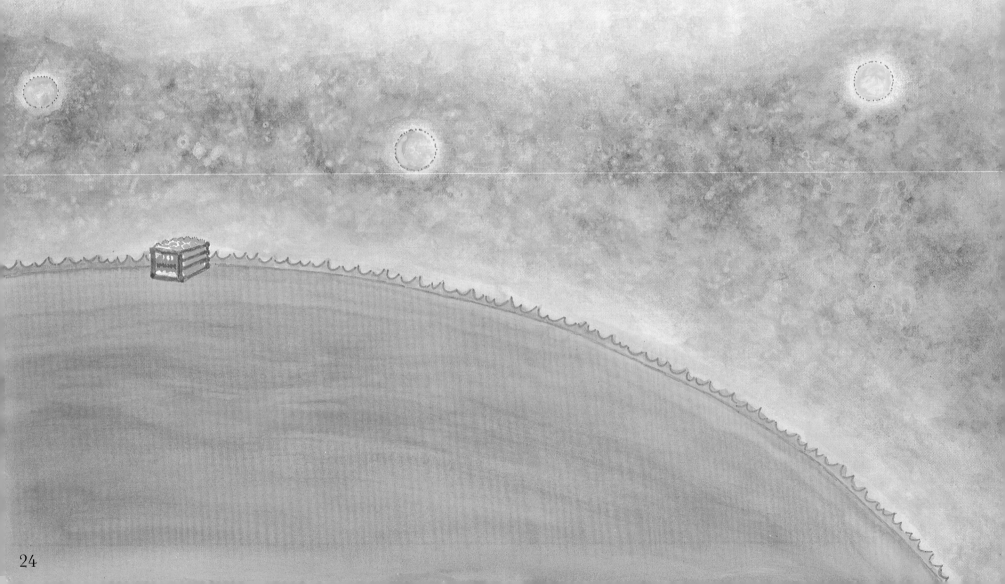

Just as a sandcastle has a shape, formed by all the grains of sand it is made of, our galaxy has a shape formed by all of its stars.

We cannot see the shape from Earth. But if we were OUTSIDE our galaxy, looking at it from a great distance, it might look something like this, with a bulging galactic centre and great cloud-like swirls glowing with the light of billions of stars! From this distance you could not see the galaxy's stars separately.

The Milky Way MUST be The Biggest Thing There Is!

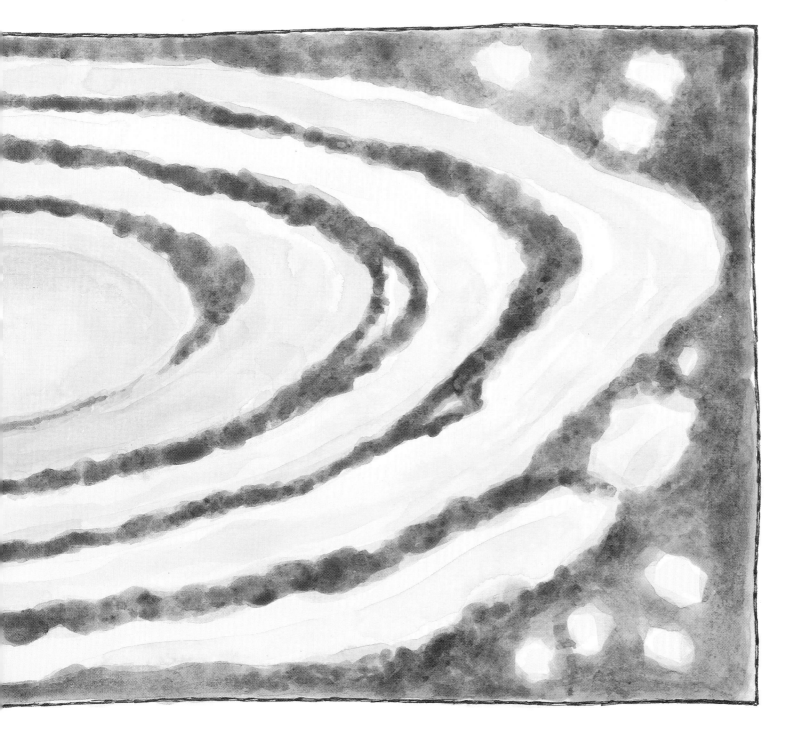

But wait.
Our galaxy
is not alone.
Astronomers,
the scientists
who study
stars, report
that there
are **BILLIONS**
of **OTHER**
galaxies out
in the
darkness we
call space.
And **ALL**
of them are
part of
Something
Even Bigger –

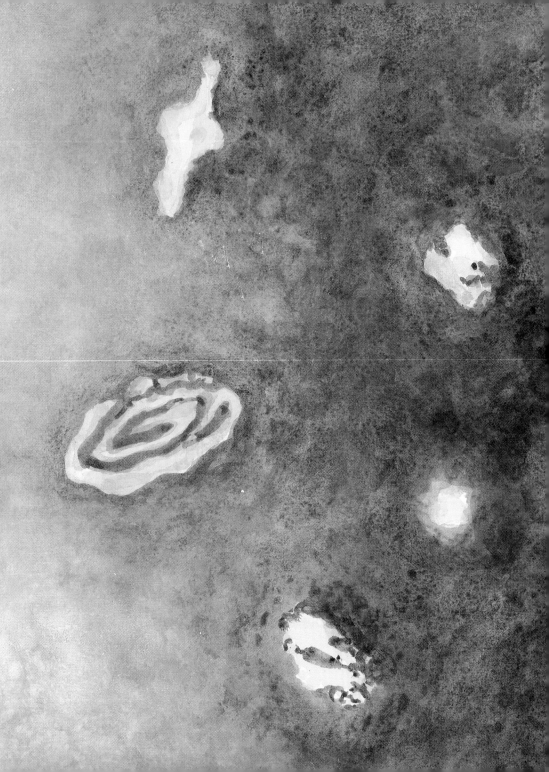

The UNIVERSE!

The UNIVERSE is
ALL THE GALAXIES
and ALL THE DARK SPACE
between them.

It is EVERYTHING THAT EXISTS
anywhere in space and time!

Because it is so
AMAZINGLY BIG,
no one knows what
the WHOLE universe
really looks like.

But here's what a tiny part of it
might look like, showing some of
the many different kinds of galaxies.

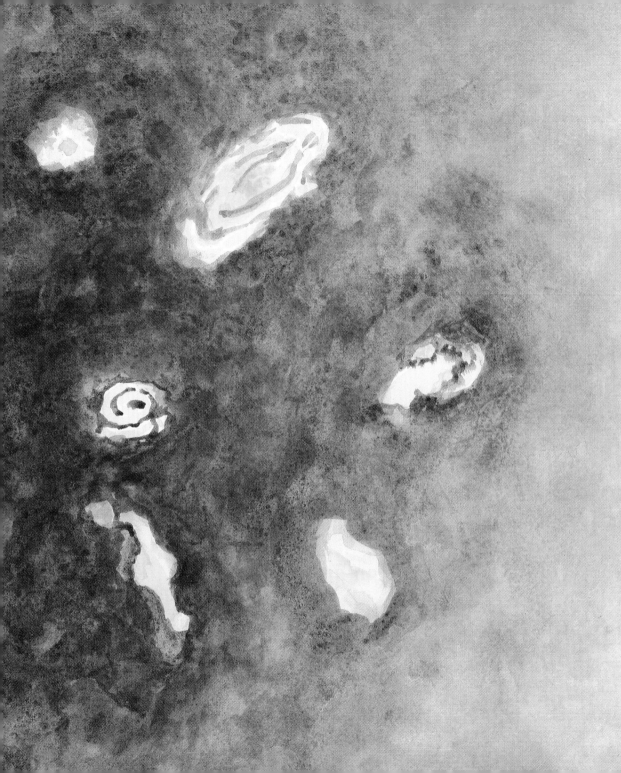

The universe is the biggest thing we know. More than likely, we can call it

THE BIGGEST THING THERE IS.

Even with our most powerful telescopes, we cannot see to the end of the universe. So we don't know how big it really is.

But this much we do know –

it's a lot bigger than a blue whale.

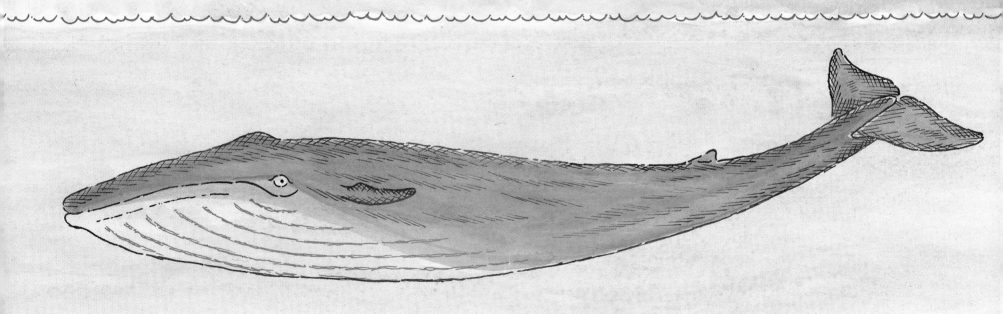

Some more thoughts on Very Big Things

It's fairly easy to imagine the size of a jar of blue whales, or a stack of Mount Everests, or even a crateful of Sun-sized oranges. But imagining the size of the universe - that's another matter.

The truth is, the universe is so unbelievably big that even with its countless billions of stars and galaxies, it is almost totally empty. Vast distances separate stars, even within those gatherings of stars we call galaxies.

If our galaxy were pictured to scale, and our Sun were the size of this dot •, the nearest star to it would be another 'dot' some 16 kilometres away, with other 'star dots' hundreds and even thousands of kilometres further away.

The distances between galaxies are also vast. Like the stars, the galaxies in this book are shown much closer together and more alike in size than they would actually be. Shrinking vast distances proved to be more practical than making this book one million kilometres wide!

Glossary

Blue whale the largest animal that has ever lived - bigger than any dinosaur! Blue whales grow to about 26 metres long and weigh about the same as twenty elephants.

Mount Everest the highest mountain on Earth. It is part of the highest mountain range - the Himalayas - which is in Asia.

Earth the planet we live on. It is one of nine planets which slowly spin or orbit around the Sun.

Star a huge ball of hot gas spinning in space.

Sun a huge star which gives light and heat to Earth.

Antares a supergiant star. It is a thousand times brighter than our Sun.

Galaxy a group of millions of stars.

Milky Way the galaxy in which our Sun and all its orbiting planets are part.